ZOOM!
Space

First published in this edition in 2004 by Cherrytree Books, a division of Evans Brothers Ltd, 2A Portman Mansions, Chiltern St, London W1U 6NR

Copyright © 2002 Orpheus Books Ltd.

Created and produced by Nicholas Harris and Claire Aston, Orpheus Books Ltd.

Text Nicholas Harris

Consultant David Hawksett, Organizer of the UK Planetary Forum

Illustrated by Sebastian Quigley *(Linden Artists)*

Other illustrators Inklink, Firenze

ISBN 1 842342 31 2

A CIP record for this book is available from the British Library.

Printed and bound in Singapore.

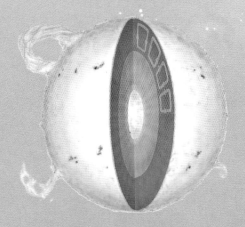

ZOOM!

Space

CHERRYTREE BOOKS

CONTENTS

LET'S ZOOM!

When you use the zoom feature on a camera, you bring pictures from distance to close-up without moving it. For example, you can capture the image of a butterfly on a leaf while keeping your distance. This book works in exactly the same way.

Imagine you were able to point a camera at the whole Universe. The illustration on pages 6 and 7 shows what you would see in your viewfinder. Now zoom in to one part of the scene. You'll see much more clearly what those spots of light look like in close-up: they're galaxies. Focus on one galaxy, keep zooming, and a few of that galaxy's billions of stars will come into view. Zoom in on one particular star with its family of planets, one very special planet (our Earth), the surface features of Earth, the rocks of which it is made . . . and eventually the minute building blocks, called atoms, which make up the rocks—and everything else in the Universe.

It's a fascinating journey through space, yet you will not have to move one millimetre! And you will discover some amazing things about space that only this incredible *zooming* book can show you . . .

UNIVERSE

The Universe is everything we know. All matter, from the tiniest grain of sand to the most gigantic star, belongs to the Universe. It even includes empty space.

Scientists think that the Universe began in an incredible explosion which happened about 15 billion years ago. During this event, called the Big Bang, all matter, energy and space were created. The Universe has expanded enormously since the Big Bang.

Matter in the Universe is not evenly spread, but clustered together in a net-like pattern. The "holes" are vast empty spaces, known as voids. The dots of light are not stars, however, but galaxies.

ZOOM DOWN INTO A SUPERCLUSTER OF GALAXIES

Barred spiral

GALAXY CLUSTER

The Universe is made of billions of galaxies, collections of stars. But galaxies are not found on their own, spread out across space. They are clumped together in clusters, themselves crowded into superclusters, giant "clouds" of galaxies that span hundreds of millions of light years. Superclusters tend to be stretched into long "strings" that link together across the Universe. In between the superclusters lie vast empty spaces, known as voids. Our own galaxy, the Milky Way, belongs to a cluster called the Local Group. It consists of about 30 galaxies.

The Local Group contains different types of galaxies: spirals (like the Milky Way), barred spirals (a little different from the spirals' catherine-wheel shape), ellipticals (shaped like ovals) and irregulars (no obvious shape). The nearest galaxy to Earth, the Large Magellanic Cloud, is 170,000 light years away.

Irregular

Spiral

GALAXY

The Milky Way Galaxy is a huge, flat spiral of stars. Named after the misty band of stars in the night sky (actually our side-on view of one of its spiral arms), it contains about 200 billion stars and measures about 100,000 light years across. It spins at 250 kilometres per second.

Nucleus

Spiral arm

The Milky Way Galaxy has a bulge at its centre, called the nucleus, where older, red stars are concentrated. Four giant arms spiral out from the nucleus. Younger blue stars are found in these arms, along with clouds of gas and dust, where new stars are forming *(see page 24)*. About half-way out from the nucleus are the middle-aged stars, mostly yellow and orange.

ZOOM DOWN INTO ONE OF THE SPIRAL ARMS

STARS

Stars produce energy (including heat and light) which they radiate in all directions as they shine. These hot, spinning globes of gas vary enormously in size and according to the amount of energy they give off. Many stars may have planets orbiting around them—some perhaps home to living things . . .

The shimmering, multi-coloured region in this illustration is known as a nebula *(see page 24)*. It is a vast cloud of dust and gas—the remains of dying stars. Some of the Galaxy's nebulae take on spectacular shapes. Nebulae provide the "raw material" from which new stars will begin to form.

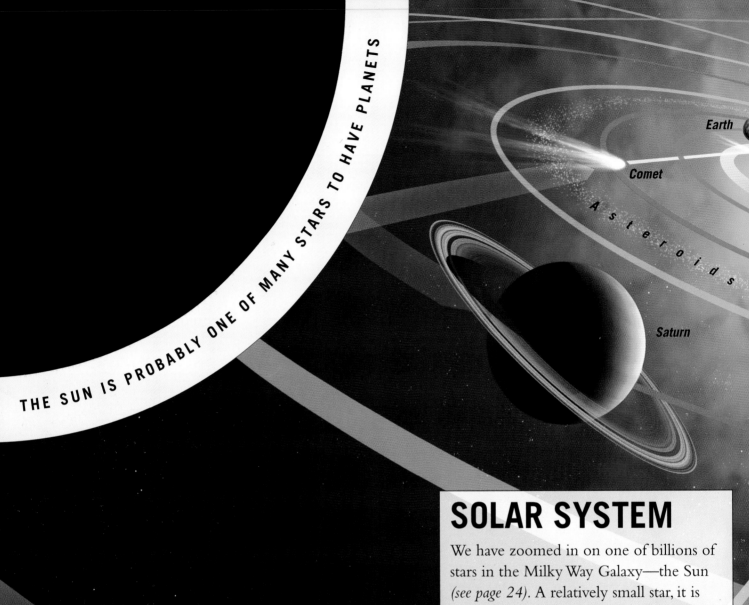

Earth

Comet

Asteroids

Saturn

Neptune

SOLAR SYSTEM

We have zoomed in on one of billions of
stars in the Milky Way Galaxy—the Sun
(see page 24). A relatively small star, it is
orbited by its family of nine planets *(see
page 26)*, which all travel around it in the
same anticlockwise direction. The Sun
and planets make up the Solar System.
This also consists of the moons (which
orbit the planets), asteroids, comets,
meteoroids and vast amounts of dust and
gas. The Sun contains more than 99% of
all the matter in the Solar System.

Sun

Mercury

Venus

Mars

Jupiter

Uranus

Pluto

IS THE THIRD NEAREST PLANET TO THE SUN

EARTH

One member of the Solar System is, of course, our own planet Earth. It is the fifth largest planet (although much smaller than the fourth largest, Neptune, *see page 27*). Earth is the only world in the Solar System known to have life, something made possible by the presence of liquid water, which covers more than 71% of its surface. Earth is also neither too close nor too far from the Sun, giving it a favourable temperature. Its atmosphere shields it from the Sun's harmful rays and protects it from bombardment by meteorites. Earth's oceans trap enough heat to avoid extremes of hot or cold.

EARTH IS A SMALL PLANET IN THE SOLAR SYSTEM

ZOOM DOWN TO A SMALL PART OF EARTH'S SURFACE

LAND

Earth's landscape appears permanent and unchanging, but it is, in fact, changing all the time. Sometimes this happens quite quickly, for example, when part of a cliff falls into the sea, or when a volcano erupts. Usually it is a very slow process.

Earth's surface is divided into giant slabs, called plates, that slide around the globe—so gradually that we cannot see them move.

Life is found nearly everywhere on Earth. Here, coniferous woodland grows on the upper mountain slopes. Roads, towns, pylons and planted fields show the influence of people.

Observatory (houses telescope)

These plate movements may cause volcanic eruptions, earthquakes and, where two plate edges collide, the crumpling up of land into mountains.

Wind, rain, frost, rivers, glaciers and the crashing of the waves all have a part to play in shaping a landscape, carving out wide valleys, gnawing away at cliffs and eventually reducing mountain ranges to level plains. People can also change a landscape. Creating reservoirs, diverting rivers and quarrying a mountain are some of the ways in which this can happen.

ZOOM DOWN TO THE GROUND TO SEE WHAT THE EARTH IS MADE OF

ROCKS

Earth is one of five planets that are chiefly made of rock. The gas giants, Jupiter, Saturn, Uranus and Neptune, have relatively small rocky cores with thick gas or liquid outer layers. Mercury, Venus, Earth and Mars all have metal cores with rocky outer layers. Pluto has an icy surface and probably a rocky core.

There are three main types of rock in Earth's crust, its outer layer. The first type, sedimentary rocks, are made from cemented rock fragments such as sand, gravel, mud or the remains of living things. Igneous rocks, the second type, are formed when magma, molten rock from the interior, rises, cools and solidifies in Earth's crust. Finally, metamorphic rocks are formed when rocks are subjected to great pressure and heat.

EARTH'S CRUST IS MADE ALMOST ENTIRELY OF ROCK

In many land areas Earth's rocky crust has a covering of soil, a mixture of rocky fragments and the rotting remains of plants and animals. Where there is soil, plants can grow.

ZOOM IN TO FIND OUT WHAT ROCKS ARE MADE OF

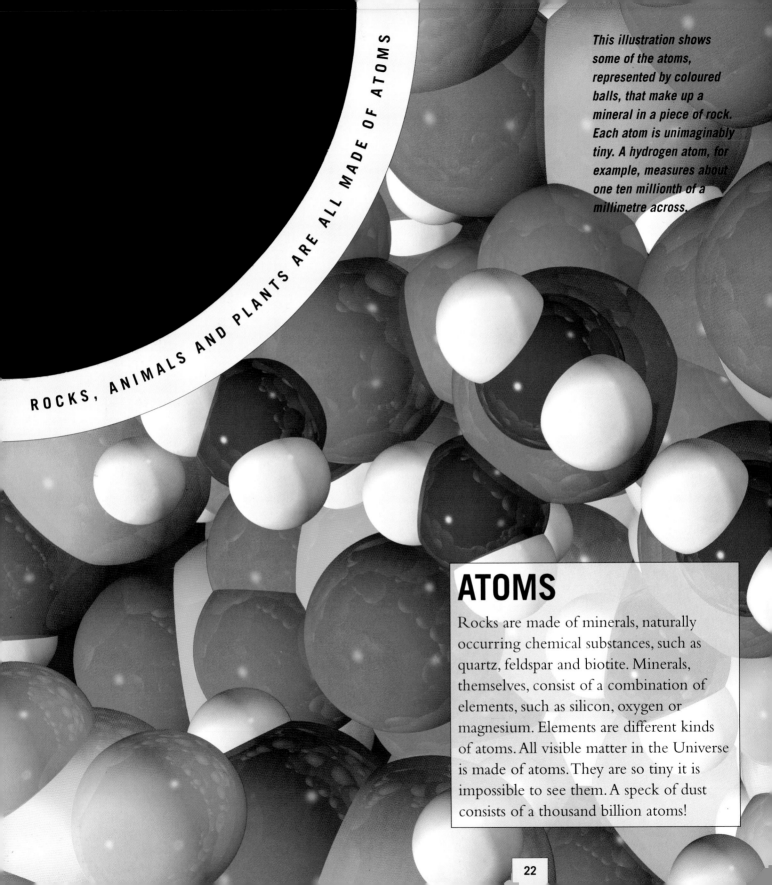

This illustration shows some of the atoms, represented by coloured balls, that make up a mineral in a piece of rock. Each atom is unimaginably tiny. A hydrogen atom, for example, measures about one ten millionth of a millimetre across.

ATOMS

Rocks are made of minerals, naturally occurring chemical substances, such as quartz, feldspar and biotite. Minerals, themselves, consist of a combination of elements, such as silicon, oxygen or magnesium. Elements are different kinds of atoms. All visible matter in the Universe is made of atoms. They are so tiny it is impossible to see them. A speck of dust consists of a thousand billion atoms!

What makes atoms different from one
another—resulting in distinct elements—
is the number of particles they each
contain. Hydrogen atoms are extremely
light because they have just two particles,
whereas lead atoms are so heavy because
they consist of many particles.

In a mineral, atoms of different elements
are linked to one another, forming
molecules. The molecules are packed
closely together, so that minerals, and the
rocks they make up, are dense solids.

STARS

Stars are giant spinning balls of hot gases. Like massive nuclear power stations, they produce vast amounts of energy in the form of heat and light which they radiate across space as they shine. Stars vary enormously in size (Betelgeuse is 1500 times the size of our own star, the Sun) and the amount of light they give off. Some of the brightest stars emit more than 100,000 times the light of the Sun, while others are 100,000 times weaker.

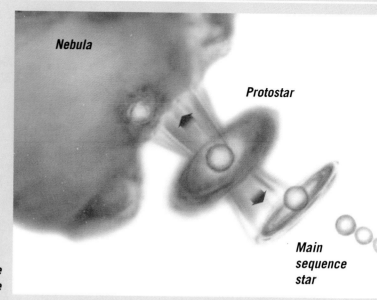

Nebula

Protostar

Main sequence star

At its centre of the Sun is the core, a region of immense pressure and heat (15 million°C). Energy produced at the Sun's core flows out through the radiative zone to the convective zone.

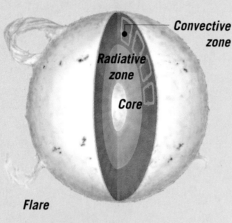

Convective zone

Radiative zone

Core

Flare

A star begins its life when clouds of dust and gas in space, known as **nebulae**, compress together under the force of gravity. Pressure from an old star exploding nearby may trigger this process. The resulting mass is called a **protostar**. Its core becomes so hot that nuclear reactions start up deep inside it. Gas and dust are blown away, although some may remain in the disc surrounding the star, eventually compressing together to form planets.

The protostar is now a **main sequence** star. Most of these stars last billions of years on the power from nuclear reactions. Eventually, however, the fuel runs out, the core collapses and the star swells into a **red giant**. A massive star will become a **supergiant** that will blast apart in a colossal explosion known as a **supernova**. It ends its days as a neutron star or a black hole *(see opposite)*.

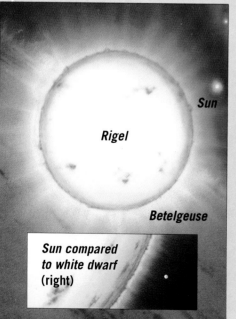

Sun

Rigel

Betelgeuse

Sun compared to white dwarf (right)

The oldest stars are swollen red giants like Betelgeuse. They are much bigger and "cooler" than young blue ones like Rigel (both stars are part of Orion). Rigel is 60 times the size of our Sun, although the Sun is itself massive when compared to the collapsed core of an old star, known as a white dwarf.

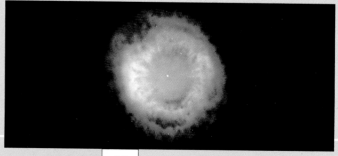

In a supernova, the exploding star shines brighter than more than one billion Suns! Chinese sky-watchers witnessed one about 950 years ago. The Crab Nebula *(right)*, a cloud of gas in the shape of a crab, is all that remains of it, apart from a tiny, super-dense **neutron star** at its centre.

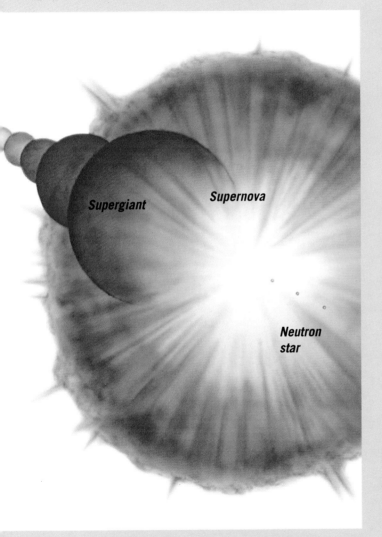

Supergiant

Supernova

Neutron star

After a supernova, the old star's core may be so dense that it collapses in on itself. It shrinks to a tiny point surrounded by a region of space where gravity is so strong that nothing—not even light—can escape from it. Scientists call these points **black holes.** Anything lying close to a black hole disappears from the Universe for good. Black holes are invisible, but it is possible to detect them. This blue star, for example, is being pulled around in a circle *(below)*. The gas torn from it forms a disc before plummeting into the black hole.

When a less massive star (like our Sun, about 7 billion years from now) runs out of fuel, it also swells up, although not on the same scale as a supergiant. After a few million years, the outer layers flake off into space, leaving behind a ring of dust and gas, known as a planetary nebula. *The Helix Nebula* (left) *is a planetary nebula. The collapsed core, no larger than a planet, is called a* white dwarf.

THE PLANETS

Mercury

Planets not to scale

Venus

Earth

Mars

Jupiter

The inner planets are dwarfed by the four "gas giants", Jupiter, Saturn, Uranus and Neptune, so-called because they chiefly consist of gas and have no solid surface. **Jupiter**, the largest planet, has patterns on its globe produced by high-speed winds and swirling storms. Its Great Red Spot is actually a giant storm—larger than Earth—that has been raging for at least 300 years.

All the gas giants have rings, but those of **Saturn** are by far the most spectacular. They are made of billions of blocks of ice and rock. **Uranus** is tilted 98° from the vertical, meaning that it orbits the Sun almost on its side. **Neptune** also has high-speed winds racing around its globe.

Icy **Pluto**, the smallest, coldest and outermost planet, has a very elongated orbit, taking it from just inside Neptune's orbit at one extreme, to billions of kilometres outside it at another.

Earth is the largest of the four inner planets: Mercury, Venus, Earth and Mars. **Mercury**, the nearest to the Sun, is heavily cratered. It has great extremes of temperature. **Venus**, permanently shrouded in thick clouds of deadly acid, has a surface temperature hotter than molten lead. Beneath the clouds, there are many volcanoes surrounded by lava plains.

Mars is the "Red Planet", so-called because of the reddish iron oxide dust that coats its surface. Channels show signs of having been carved by running water, meaning that there may possibly once have been life on Mars.

PLANET	DIAMETER	DAY measured in Earth days or hours	YEAR measured in Earth days or years	AVERAGE DISTANCE FROM SUN	SURFACE TEMPERATURE	MOONS
Mercury	4878 km	58.6 days	88 days	58 million km	–170 to +350°C	none
Venus	12,103 km	243 days	225 days	108 million km	490°C	none
Earth	12,756 km	23 hrs 56 min	365.26 days	149.6 million km	–70 to +55°C	1
Mars	6794 km	24.6 hours	687 days	228 million km	–137 to +26°C	2
Jupiter	142,884 km	9.8 hours	11.8 years	778 million km	–150°C	28
Saturn	120,536 km	10.2 hours	29.4 years	1427 million km	–180°C	30
Uranus	51,118 km	17.2 hours	84 years	2869 million km	–210°C	21
Neptune	50,538 km	16.1 hours	164.8 years	4497 million km	–220°C	8
Pluto	2324 km	6.4 days	248 years	5906 million km	–220°C	1

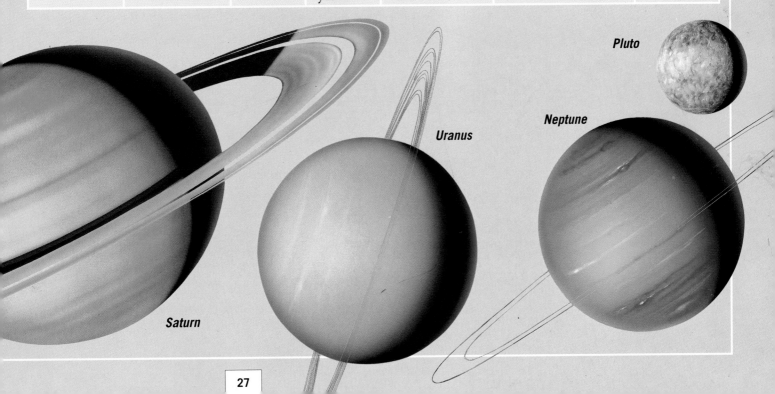

Pluto

Neptune

Uranus

Saturn

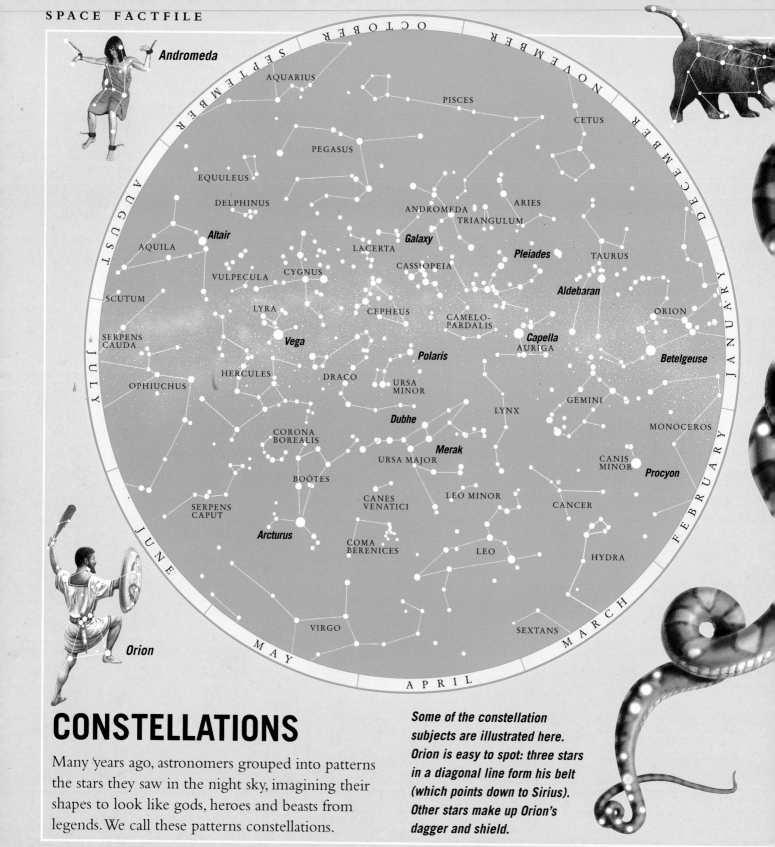

CONSTELLATIONS

Many years ago, astronomers grouped into patterns the stars they saw in the night sky, imagining their shapes to look like gods, heroes and beasts from legends. We call these patterns constellations.

Some of the constellation subjects are illustrated here. Orion is easy to spot: three stars in a diagonal line form his belt (which points down to Sirius). Other stars make up Orion's dagger and shield.

28

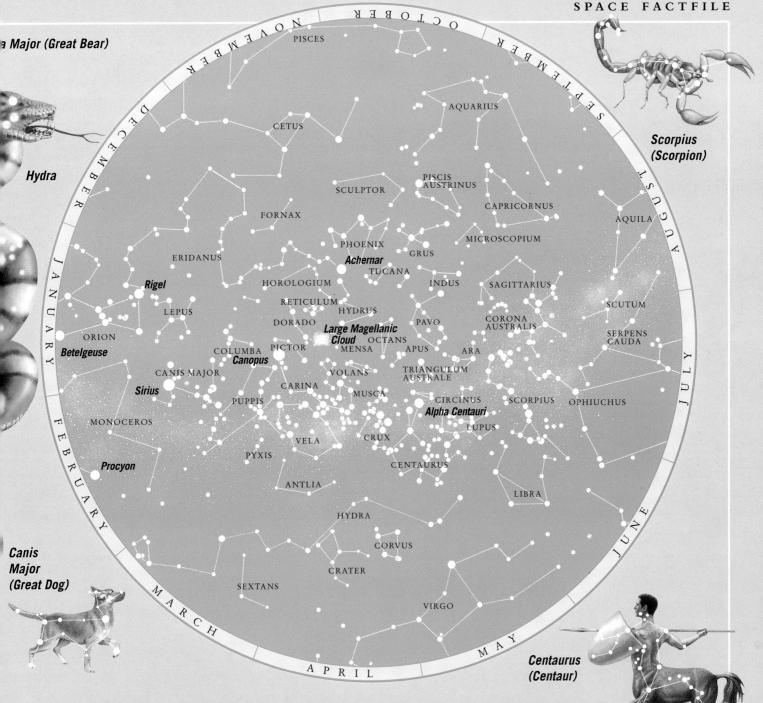

Major (Great Bear)

Hydra

Scorpius (Scorpion)

Canis Major (Great Dog)

Centaurus (Centaur)

The 88 constellations include 48 known to the ancient Greeks. European explorers sailing the southern seas later added others visible only in southern hemisphere skies. Constellations are useful for locating certain stars and galaxies. Two of the brightest stars in Ursa Major, for example, point to Polaris, almost exactly due north.

To use these charts, turn the book around so the present month is at the bottom. Then, at 10.00 pm, face south (northern hemisphere) or north (southern hemisphere) to locate the constellations on the chart.

GLOSSARY

Asteroid A rocky body that orbits the Sun. Asteroids range in size from tiny specks to just under 1000 kilometres in diameter.

Atmosphere The envelope of gases that surrounds a planet, moon or star.

Atom A basic building block of matter. Elements, naturally occurring substances like hydrogen, carbon or gold that cannot be broken down into simpler substances, are each made up from atoms of the same kind.

Big Bang The origin of the Universe, which took place in a gigantic explosion from an incredibly hot and dense state about 15 billion years ago.

Black hole A region of space from which nothing, not even light, can escape. Its force of gravity is much more powerful than any normal star.

Comet An object made of dust and ice that orbits the Sun. On nearing the Sun, it develops two immensely long tails streaming away from the Sun.

Constellation A group of stars forming a pattern in the night sky.

Galaxy An enormous cluster of stars, planets, gas and dust. Galaxies may contain billions of stars. They are, themselves, gathered together in clusters of up to a few thousand.

Light year The distance that light, which moves at a speed of about 300,000 kilometres per second, travels in one year. Astronomers use light years to measure the immense distances in space

Meteorite A meteoroid that falls from space to land on to the surface of a planet or a moon.

Meteoroid Rocks or dust particles that orbit round the Sun. Many meteoroids were once parts of asteroids. When a meteoroid burns up close to Earth it is known as a **meteor**.

Molecule A combination of atoms of different types bonded together. A molecule is the smallest part of a substance that can exist by itself and still possess its chemical properties.

Moon A smaller object that orbits a planet, also known as a natural satellite.

Nebula A cloud of gas or dust in space.

Orbit The circular or elliptical (oval-shaped) path followed by one object round another. For example, the Moon orbits Earth, while Earth orbits the Sun.

Particle, subatomic The constituent parts of an atom. They include electrons and the protons and neutrons found in the atomic nucleus (centre).

Planet A world that orbits a star. Planets do not radiate their own light, but reflect it from the star.

Plates, tectonic The large slabs into which Earth's surface is divided.

Solar System The Solar System consists of the Sun, together with the nine planets, their moons, comets, asteroids, meteoroids and a mass of gas and dust that all circle around it.

Star A globe of gas that produces heat from nuclear reactions inside its core and radiates light from its hot surface.

Supernova The massive explosion of a supergiant star.

Universe All matter and space.

INDEX